THE WRITER'S LITTLE INSTRUCTION BOOK

385 Secrets for Writing Well & Getting Published

The Writer's Little Instruction Book

385 Secrets for Writing Well & Getting Published

Paul Raymond Martin

Illustrations by Polly Keener

Writer's World Press
Aurora, Ohio

Writer's World Press, 35 N. Chillicothe Road, Suite D, Aurora, Ohio 44202
Telephone: 330/562-6667, E-mail: WritersWorld@juno.com

Publisher's Cataloging-in-Publications

Martin, Paul Raymond.
    The writer's little instruction book : 385 secrets for writing
well & getting published / Paul Raymond Martin ; illustrations:
Polly Keener. -- 1st ed.
    p. cm.
    Includes index.
    Preassigned LCCN: 97-62093
    ISBN: 0-9631441-7-0

    1. Authorship--Miscellanea.   I. Keener, Polly, 1946- II.
Title.
PN153.M378 1998   808'.02
                                        QB197-41367

for

Mom and Dad,

who gave me the gift of life

ACKNOWLEDGMENTS

A hug from my heart and a thank-you smile to:

The graduate assistant in freshman composition at Carnegie-Mellon University, for counseling me to "Keep doing what you're doing." Dearest friends and family, for allowing me the time and personal space to write. Fellow writers, for providing inspiration and instruction. Magazine, newsletter and anthology editors galore, for encouraging and publishing my work. Lavern Hall, my editor and publisher, for pursuing excellence in every phase of publication. Kathie Westerfield, for never doubting me.

Portions of this manuscript have been published, in somewhat different form, in *Creativity Connection, Fiction Writer's Guideline, Gotta Write Network LitMag, Paperless Planet, Smile, Writer's International Forum* and *Writer's Keeper.*

CONTENTS

INTRODUCTION

My niece, Diane Sharp, started it all by sending me a book of aphorisms as a holiday gift. As I flipped through the little book, several items caught my eye. Rather than set the book aside, I turned to page one and began reading. The wisdom offered rang true enough, for life in general, but not quite apt for my life as a writer. I began to pay more attention to expressions of wisdom and humor, and how they related to writing. In time, I began to express the writing lessons I was learning, or re-learning, in the same format. As my list of aphorisms grew, I shared them with other writers.

Now it's your turn. I invite you to turn to page one and begin reading.

PAUL RAYMOND MARTIN

Chapter One
INSPIRATION FOR WRITERS

You Gotta Keep Your Saw in the Wood

You can't build a reputation on what you're going to do.

Henry Ford

Talking is a hydrant in the yard
and writing is a faucet upstairs in the house.
Opening the first takes all the pressure off the second.

Robert Frost

It's been said that
literature is a high form of gossip.
Heard any good stuff lately?
Do tell!

In writing
(as in most endeavors)
there is always room for excellence.

In writing
(as in most endeavors)
sweat rules over inspiration.

What some folks call genius
is simply intelligence and awareness,
applied with discipline.

We write best
what we need most to understand.

We write in order to maintain
our connectedness with all things
great and small—
past, present and future.

Your best writing will come
of wondering and questioning,
rather than of knowing and answering.

 Identify your greatest strength,
your most troubling weakness,
your most persistent fear,
your most problematic issue,
your most turbulent emotion.
Now write.

Write with major intent.
Nothing less will do.

Begin each day's writing
with whatever you most want to write about.

See life as it is,
but write about life as it might be.

Trust yourself to generate new writing ideas
tomorrow
and the next day
and the next.

Write what you care about
    and you will evoke emotion.
Write what you know about
    and you will build credibility.
Write what you would like to know about
    and you will discover your truth.

Fear of failure,
fear of success:
If you give in to it,
it's all the same.

You will never overcome your fear
that your writing is insipid
or incomprehensible or trivial—
write in spite of the fear.

The world wide web
may offer a superhighway of information
and opinion, even a sense of community.
But writing remains a self-made path
into the unknown.

Your writing must be as honest
as your courage allows.

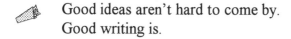 Good ideas aren't hard to come by.
Good writing is.

Writing is not about ideas,
it is about the expression of ideas—
a written expression.

You cannot decide once-and-for-all to be a writer.
You must renew your commitment to writing every day.

What other people say about your writing
may affect your writing
but never your commitment to your writing.

Never...
talk yourself out of a story.
Instead, write the story out of yourself.

Never...
use your writing
as fodder for small talk.
It is more important than that
and deserves better.

Newspaper editors refer
to syndicated material as "furniture."
So build yourself a comfortable couch.

Give yourself time
to develop as a writer.
Be patient with yourself.

We write poorly
in order to learn
to write well.

If you came to writing later in life than most,
glory in it.
You have a perspective and appreciation of life
unavailable to you earlier.

You didn't start writing earlier
because you weren't ready.
You had other priorities and lessons to learn.
Now, you are ready.

Do not be concerned
that the reader be moved by all your words,
rather that the reader be moved
by your words at all.

Writing well is tedious.
Having written well is joyful.

The road to unfinished work
is paved with good intentions.

The road to published work
is always under construction.

You put words on paper.
You teach,
you inform,
you motivate,
you entertain,
you evoke.
The whole world envies you.

Every word you write is a decision.
The more decisions you make, the easier they become.

As the old-time lumberjacks used to say,
"You gotta keep your saw in the wood."

Chapter Two
CHARACTERIZATION

Every Memorable Character Has a Wart

*It is not in the still calm of life, or in the repose of a pacific station,
that great characters are formed...
Great necessities call out great virtues.*

Abigail Adams

*We must have a weak spot or two in a character
before we can love it much.*

Oliver Wendell Holmes, Sr.

Still waters may run deep,
but still characters are just still.

 Develop empathy toward others in your everyday life.
You'll need it to develop characters in your writing life.

 Main characters must act,
not be acted upon.

 Your main character's ability to resolve problems
should be hampered, but the task not made impossible,
by his or her frailties.

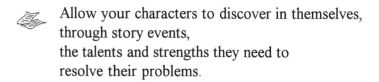 Allow your characters to discover in themselves,
through story events,
the talents and strengths they need to
resolve their problems.

Develop your main character as someone with whom
you would enjoy spending a great deal of time—
because you will.

When choosing a point-of-view character,
ask yourself, "Who is the reader supposed to be?"

Define your characters carefully,
for they will in turn define
the breadth of your work.

 You don't have to like every character you create.
Shouldn't, in fact.
But you must be awfully curious about them.

 Study ordinary people
in order to create extraordinary characters.

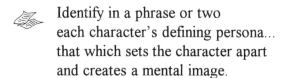 Identify in a phrase or two
each character's defining persona...
that which sets the character apart
and creates a mental image.

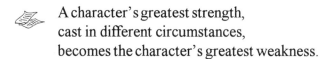 A character's greatest strength,
cast in different circumstances,
becomes the character's greatest weakness.

Good characters have their weaknesses,
evil characters have their strengths.
And both have their reasons.

Like everyday folks,
characters must be in enough pain
to make a change in their lives.

 Every character changes the story.
Every story changes the character.

 Even in a short story,
time must pass
for characters to change believably.

Just as in real life...
characters disdain in others
what they cannot abide in themselves.

 Just as in real life...
the most difficult decisions for characters
are those in which each alternative
promises both good and bad outcomes.

Just like you and me...
well-drawn characters carry with them
the emotional and psychological baggage
of their pasts.

 Just like you and me...
characters' behavior follows a pattern:
we feel, we think, we act—
though sometimes we skip the second part.

In fiction there are no selfless acts:
Even the most altruistic character
acts as he or she must
in order to feel good
and to be at peace.

 Your character's way of thinking,
as well as the thoughts themselves,
help to define character.
From time to time, let the reader sneak a peek
into the character's thought process.

During dialogue and internal monologues,
provide your characters with "stage business,"
trivial but distinctive actions, e.g., adjusting the blinds,
browsing through a magazine or retying boot laces.

 You may love your characters.
You may hate your characters.
You may NOT feel indifferent toward your characters.

 The writer must know exactly how each character feels,
even if the character doesn't.

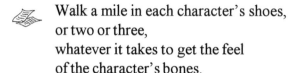 Walk a mile in each character's shoes,
or two or three,
whatever it takes to get the feel
of the character's bones.

Even the most cerebral of characters
are at their most endearing
when they act on the basis of emotion
rather than intellect.

Your most engaging characters will rise
from the dust and detritus of personal experience.

An attentive writer is midwife,
nanny, uncle and undertaker
to the story's characters.

 By the end of the story,
the reader should know
the main characters well enough
to carry on the storyline.

 In most stories,
the antagonist writes the problem,
the protagonist writes the resolution.

It's been said
that "fiction is life dressed up for a party."
And the writer controls the guest list.

 Writing is like acting,
except the writer gets to play all the parts.

 Create each character in your head,
then give just enough information
for the reader to do the same.

In developing your characters,
comfort the afflicted and afflict the comfortable.

 If your characters are having more fun than you are,
you're on the right track.

 Think of your characters as moving in a force field:
being pulled this way and that
as they move toward their respective goals.

 Every memorable character has a wart, of sorts.

Chapter Three
DIALOGUE

Reading Is A Lot Like Eavesdropping

The pen is the tongue of the mind.

Miguel de Cervantes

Literature is news that stays news.

Ezra Pound

📚 Characters are able to say things
on the spur of the moment
the way we wish we could in real life.

📚 Good dialogue is artfully concise.

📚 Dialogue creates
white space on the page,
making the book easier to read
and more approachable.

In fiction, nothing is as dull or as useless as a dialogue of agreement.

In fiction and in real life, one-on-one dialogue works best.

Diction, not dialect.

Dialect is difficult to write and an imposition on the reader.

Skinny the narrative and fatten the dialogue.

Well-written dialogue
is efficient stuff:
it reveals character,
lends realism
and advances the plot.

Well-written dialogue,
especially the main character's,
becomes the reader's own words.

Tape record and transcribe, verbatim,
an everyday conversation.
Compare it with well-written dialogue.
Straight away, you'll see the difference.

To test for variance in voice
among your characters,
remove the "he saids" and "she saids."
Can you tell who is speaking
by the diction and cadence of the dialogue?

To get into the flow of writing dialogue,
imagine what a close friend or relative
would say in a given situation.
And <u>how</u>.

Read your work aloud, especially dialogue.
Listen for cadence and rhythm and breathing.

Many readers skip long narrative passages
to "get to the good stuff"—
what characters say and do to each other.
Do the same as you write.

Unlike real life...
each character's dialogue must serve a purpose.

Unlike real life...
one character never tells another
what the latter already
knows.

Unlike real life...
characters mention the weather
only if it is relevant or portentous.

Avoid using adverbs to attribute dialogue.
Well-written dialogue will speak for itself.

In attributing dialogue, "said" is all that needs to be said.

Cliches may be used in dialogue to further characterization,
but never in narration.

Carry a notepad to write down the good stuff
as soon as you overhear it.

Reading good dialogue is a lot like eavesdropping.
No wonder readers love it!

Get Your Character Out of the Tree

Persons attempting to find a motive in this narrative will be prosecuted; persons attempting to find a moral in it will be banished; persons attempting to find a plot in it will be shot.

Mark Twain

Surely it was time someone invented a new plot, or that the author came out from the bushes.

Virginia Woolf

A single well-cast scene will reveal more
than an encyclopedia of narration.

 Each scene should be a microcosm of the story whole:
a problem introduced, heightened and resolved.
In other words, something must change.

 Every big scene should include a ticking clock,
in a figurative sense.
The protagonist must do something...RIGHT NOW!

In well-written work,
the reader will act out the big scenes,
moment by moment.

 The story problem must be resolved by the protagonist
through willful choices and actions,
not by an act of nature or the intervention
of other characters.

 The more obstacles the protagonist overcomes
in resolving problems, the better the story
and the better readers will like it,
especially if the obstacles are varied
and increasingly difficult.

The worse things get for your hero or heroine,
the sweeter the triumph for your readers.

 Be cruel to your characters.
Push them until they absolutely must take action.

 Unlike everyday life,
things don't "just happen" in fiction.
What happens must grow out of the characters' wants
and resources.

In fiction, everything happens for a reason.
(Some people believe this is true in real life, too.)

In your everyday life, avoid trouble.
In your writing life, revel in it.

In writing,
as in real life,
everything relates to everything,
only more so.

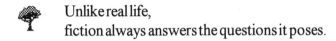 Unlike real life,
fiction always answers the questions it poses.

Motive is the linchpin between character and plot.
Characters' motives drive the action.

Plot gets readers involved;
characterization makes them care.

Plot requires more than a mere sequence of events;
it requires a causal sequence of events.

Well-constructed plots seem inevitable.
The story just couldn't have turned out any differently,
even if there were numerous twists and
an unexpected ending.

 Until you decide the story is finished, plot is tentative.

 Plots are found as theme unfolds to the writer.
Themes are found as plot unfolds to the reader.

 Fear little
if plot detail is not clear when you begin writing;
fear much if it is.

If you cannot summarize your story in a sentence, you probably are writing more than one story.

 There are three themes in most fiction:
life is a struggle,
humans are resilient,
and effort will triumph.

 Story is what happens. Plot is how and why.

 Get your character up a tree.
Put tigers under the tree.
Get your character out of the tree.

Chapter Five
STYLE

Write Against the Wind

*The original writer is not one who imitates nobody,
but one whom nobody can imitate.*

Francois Rene de Chateaubriand

*He writes so well he makes me feel like
putting my quill back in my goose.*

Fred Allen

Writing is making the same mistake
over and over
until you learn
to not make that particular mistake
anymore.

Find
   the confidence
      to write simply.

Whisper
   your observations
      onto the page.

Style is best when wholly unnoticed by the reader.

Talent is a matter of genetics.
Style is a matter of practice.

Never make the reader aware of being told a story,
unless the narrator is also a character.

You know you've written well when readers say,
"Oh, I could have written that!"

If a piece is really well-written,
no one notices the writing.

If the reader becomes aware of style or technique,
the writer is getting in the way.

Diction is the currency of writing.
It is the medium of exchange
and evidence of literary worth.

Every fiction writer should compose poetry;
it sharpens imagery and disciplines diction.

The diction required to write children's stories
is akin to that required to write poetry.

In fiction, as in real life,
what is suggested
is far more powerful
than what is revealed.

Good description capitalizes on all the senses.

Create as does a child,
without concern for
what others may think
or whether it's been done before.

Nouns and verbs
are movers and shakers,
the power words of language.

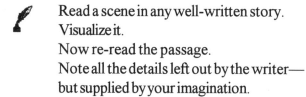

Read a scene in any well-written story.
Visualize it.
Now re-read the passage.
Note all the details left out by the writer—
but supplied by your imagination.

Readers hold each scene in suspended animation,
reshaping the scene as details are revealed.
To painstakingly set up each scene
is to distrust and disparage the reader.

The reader (and the critics)
will always see more than you wrote.

Like today's computer systems,
today's fiction is icon-based.
Readers crave images over narration.

A well-crafted first paragraph should
"put a worry on a body."

It's okay for a character to show off.
It's not okay for a writer to show off.

If you manage to move yourself as you write,
whether to laughter or tears,
anguish or joy,
chances are your work also will move the reader.

In good fiction,
truth is seldom implied
but often inferred.

Start with yourself and write outward.

Discover an emotional truth within yourself.
Present it to your readers.
Therein lies your voice.

A writer's voice is not found; it evolves.

A writer must have something to say
and a voice with which to say it.

Take risks in your writing.
If not there,
where?

"Better safe than sorry" in living.
"Safe is sorry" in writing.

Trust your instincts.
Trust your observations.
Trust your judgments.
Trust your voice.

You may hide from strong feelings in your everyday life,
but not in your writing.

Writing about painful subjects
is less painful
than not writing about them.

Strive not to create good writing but good reading.

Handle your words as carefully
as you handle your money.

Economy renders significance.

For every rule of thumb,
there is always an insolent pinky finger
that does its own thing.

Don't worry about using a lot of big words
to impress the reader.
People who know the big words
also know the small words.

Carving a story is just the opposite of carving a turkey:
cut away everything that isn't essential
and keep the carcass.

Early drafts are generous; polished drafts are stingy.

One's style,
be it pedantic,
engaging or boorish,
has about the same effect in writing as in conversation.

Think of your story
as if each scene
were to be
illustrated,
for that is exactly
what the reader does.

Internal monologues should be about as long
as the character's nose.

Beware the Land of the Ing's!

Good writing, frogs and arguments can be dissected, but none ever survives the process.

The more constrained a writer is by word count, the better the writing.

Develop an eye for detail.
And an ear.
And a nose.
And a taste and feel as well.

Write against the wind.

Chapter Six
TECHNIQUE

Dead Men Tell No Tales

I write from the worm's eye point of view.

Ernie Pyle

Every novel should have a beginning, a muddle, and an end.
The "muddle" is the heart of your tale.

Attributed to Peter De Vries

✳Remember this page.

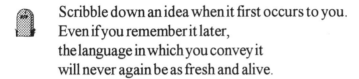

Scribble down an idea when it first occurs to you.
Even if you remember it later,
the language in which you convey it
will never again be as fresh and alive.

Write the first draft as fast as you can.

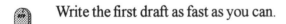

Start in the middle of things.

Begin your story with <u>conflict</u> rather than <u>description</u>.

 The beginning of a story
is the writer's first chance
to make a good impression
and the ending
is the writer's last chance
to make a lasting impression.

 Think of the beginning of your story
as if it were an opening gambit
in approaching an attractive person
at a cocktail party.

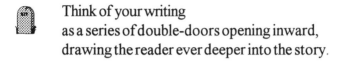 Think of your writing
as a series of double-doors opening inward,
drawing the reader ever deeper into the story.

Every paragraph,
every sentence,
every word
must carry its weight,
must do a job.

Provide enough detail
to stimulate the reader's imagination,
then get out of the way.

If you get everything else wrong,
but move the reader with your emotion,
you have succeeded.

Conflict among choices of the mind
    may intrigue the reader.
Conflict among choices of the heart
    will involve the reader.

Actors ask of the director,
"What is my motivation in this scene?"
Characters ask the same of the writer.

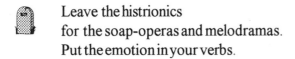 Leave the histrionics
for the soap-operas and melodramas.
Put the emotion in your verbs.

In real life,
there is no authorial voice-over
announcing people's motives and emotions.
Nor should there be in fiction.

A sex scene,
like any other,
must reveal character
and advance the plot.

To keep readers revved up,
make things worse for your main character
(preferably much worse)
before things get better.

 Rule of thumb:
your main character should fail twice
to resolve the story problem,
then succeed.

Most of today's readers demand immediate gratification. The writer must pose and resolve one conflict after another enroute to resolving the main story problem.

In a well-crafted story,
the reader knows life will never again
be the same for the main character
and perhaps,
for the reader as well.

Always play fair:
Both the protagonist <u>and</u> the antagonist
must be allowed
to use their talents and resources fully
to try to get what they want.

Always play fair:
The reader gets to know
everything the point-of-view character knows.

During moments of high conflict or emotional intensity,
our powers of observation are heightened,
our mental camera records everything in exacting detail
and present the scene in excruciating slow motion.
The same is true in story life, but remember—
only during moments of great intensity.

In real life,
most "scenes" don't change much of anything.
In story life,
every scene changes something.

In real life,
events of the day
sometimes foreshadow future developments.
In story life,
they always do.

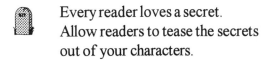

Every reader loves a secret.
Allow readers to tease the secrets
out of your characters.

Readers insist that everything tie together in a novel
precisely because things rarely do so in real life.

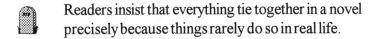

Put the qualifiers up front.
End each sentence with a <u>punch.</u>

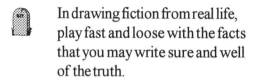

In drawing fiction from real life,
play fast and loose with the facts
that you may write sure and well
of the truth.

Some writers outline before they begin.
Some dive right in and write.
Whatever your approach,
be sure to outline at some point.

Use a thesaurus, if you must,
to remind yourself of the right word,
not to impose one.

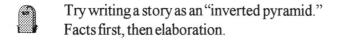

Try writing a story as an "inverted pyramid."
Facts first, then elaboration.

Choose as your point-of-view character
the person most at risk in the story.

If you shift point-of-view
or alter time sequences
or employ dialect
or use esoteric language
or do anything
that makes the work more difficult to read,
be sure you gain more than you lose.

Never waste your reader's time.

 If a flashback runs on too long
or isn't wholly relevant,
it becomes a flopback.

 Test for your story opening:
If you were waiting in line at the checkout stand
and you read the first few paragraphs of the story,
would you buy the magazine?

When the writer stops to describe something, the reader stops, too.

 The primary rule of good story-telling: "Get on with it!"

 "Dead men tell no tales," notes the proverb. And point-of-view characters never die.

Chapter Seven
WRITER'S BLOCK

Write About Your Secret Life

There is nothing to write about, you say.
Well then, write and let me know just this—
that there is nothing to write about.

Pliny the Younger

If you wait for inspiration,
you're not a writer, but a waiter.

Anonymous

A negative attitude will erode
your creative landscape
more surely than a torrent of criticism.

Writers make words.
Wannabes make excuses.

Writing is the only known cure for not writing.

 Sit down.
Write a sentence.
Now write another sentence.
Write as many as you need to
until the good stuff comes.

 There is no penalty for lousy first drafts.

Give some air-time to the critics in your head,
if you must,
then tell them to shut up and listen while you write.

You needn't be in control
of your material
to begin writing—
only to finish.

Write about what's inside you.
What makes you angry, tearful, joyful, peaceful?

Don't fret overmuch about the title,
or let that keep you from starting.
The title is the item editors
most often change anyway.

 It is important to offer readers
a crackerjack opening,
but it's rarely the first sentence written.

 Don't worry about starting at the beginning.
Just start.
The beginning will reveal itself as you write.

Start with whatever you have:
a scene, a snatch of dialogue, a character's mannerism.
You can fill in and sort it out later.

 Start with whatever part of the story
you most want to write
and write as much as you can about it.
Write forward and backward
from your starting point.

 Write quickly, open the door to your subconscious
before your internal editor can take control.

Write down the first three ideas that comes to mind, but don't make a promise to use any of them.

 Write for an audience of one:
an intelligent-but-uninformed friend
with whom you choose to share
a part of yourself.

 Write half-a-dozen screaming headlines for your article, then rewrite the article using each headline as a new slant.

Write a cover blurb for your story—
as if it were being published as a mass market paperback.

Work on more than one piece of writing at a time.
When one stalls, move to another.

It's alright
to allow an idea to percolate for awhile.
It's not alright
to excuse yourself from putting the idea on paper.

Reading, meditation, beautiful settings,
music, art, exercise, rest, sex,
certain foods or beverages:
any of these may stimulate your creativity.
Find out what works for you.

Write About Your Secret Life

 If you're stuck, write a letter to a friend
explaining what you're trying to write.

 If you're having trouble getting started,
set the kitchen timer and write for fifteen minutes.
✳ You can do anything for fifteen minutes.
Some days, you won't hear the timer ring.

 If for a time you can't write well, write poorly.
You can fix it later or throw it away.

 It is better to write poorly
than to not write at all.

Keep a journal:
bits of dialogue that catch your ear,
clothes or signs or business names that catch your eye,
incidents in the grocery store,
mannerisms of everyday people,
apt phrases, "what-if" questions...

 Consider what you would most like to do,
if you dared.
Now do it through your characters.

When you finish a writing session,
leave off with a specific question
to be answered in the next scene or section,
or a one-sentence summary of what happens next.

 Write the part of the story
you wouldn't show your mother.

 Write about your secret life.
The one you live in your head.

Chapter Eight
EDITING
Fail Your Way To Success

The beautiful part of writing is that you don't have to get it right the first time, unlike, say, a brain surgeon.

Robert Cromier

Nature fits all her children with something to do. He who would write and can't write, can surely review.

James Russell Lowell

The most useful skill
a writer can acquire
is the ability to edit one's work...RUTHLESSLY.

Indulge yourself when you write,
but not when you re-write.

Write from the creative hemisphere of your brain.
Edit from the analytical hemisphere.

When you are inundated by an emotional tidal wave,
pour it out on paper.
Then distance yourself from it for a time
and begin anew,
but keep the power of what you wrote earlier.

When you finish writing a piece,
delete the first paragraph.
Now read the story again.
Does it make a difference?
If not, try deleting the first page
or the first few pages.

If you are terribly fond
of a particular passage in your manuscript,
almost surely it does not belong.

Imagine you are about to fax your story at $10 per word.
Now edit.

Be miserly toward your words
so that editors won't be.

Root out the superfluous and the valueless,
lest your flowers be lost among the weeds.

Let a "finished" piece rest for at least a week,
then re-edit it—
as if it were someone else's work.

If a passage doesn't work,
the fault is not with the reader.

If you get bored writing a part of the story,
pity the reader. Dump it.

If a reader whose opinion you value
doesn't finish reading your story,
ask the reader to show you
where he or she left off reading,
so you can re-write that passage.

In fiction, "then" is superfluous.
The reader knows what is written next, happens next.

In real estate, it's "location, location, location."
In writing, it's "diction, diction, diction."

Make revision a way of life.

Proofread your finished work at least twice,
especially if you use an electronic spell-checker.

Listen to critiques, but
—first and last—
please yourself.

Re-writing is never finished,
but at some point you have to let it be,
and send it out to market.

Good writers make more mistakes than poor writers—
especially mistakes correcting mistakes.

The numbers of typographical errors
varies directly with the creative force
of the writing—
also with sleep deprivation.

Practice may improve your writing.
Examined practice will surely improve your writing.

Better to write one superb sentence
than a hundred mediocre ones.

Each rejection slip
gives you an opportunity
to improve your work.
If it no longer pleases you,
or if an editor's comments ring true,
change the work.

The first rule of writing
  is to write.
The second rule of writing
  is to re-write.
The third rule of writing
  is the same as the second.

Rewrite from several starting points,
not just the beginning.

No matter how poorly written a piece,
there is always something to build on.
No matter how well written a piece,
there is always a way to make it better.

The key to effective writing
is not so much getting words on paper
as it is getting words off paper.

Whatever you're writing,
the work always plays better in your head
than it does on paper.
Fortunately, it also plays better in the reader's head.

Thomas Edison said,
"I fail my way to success."
Writers, too.

Chapter Nine

MARKETING

No Fair Hiding Stuff in the Drawer

Write out of love, write out of instinct, write out of reason. . . .
But always for money.

Louis Untermeyer

A good many young writers make the mistake of enclosing a stamped,
self-addressed envelope, big enough for the manuscript to come
back in. This is too much of a temptation to the editor.

Ring Lardner

No writer was ever born published.

Every published writer
has produced some unsalable work.

If you're "not writing for publication,"
you're writing a diary.

Never...
excuse your work as "just a draft."

Never...
attempt to explain your work.
Either it's on the page or it's not.

Write as well as you can,
say what you have to say...
then find a market for your work.

For the emerging writer,
marketing is at least half the job
of creating publishable work...
the dark half.

When you market your writing,
you are in sales.
Think accordingly.
Act accordingly.

Everything you do
to gain favorable notice for your work
is part of marketing.

As effective as you may be in marketing,
your writing will speak most powerfully for you.
Powerful writing will not, however, market itself.

A well-written book may be rejected
simply because an agent or publisher
cannot project a sufficient market for it.

Editors are not the enemy.
They want the same thing you want.

Editors always want more of the same,
only different.

In most publishing houses,
an editor's job is to acquire publishable work,
not to create it.

Editors read all day and half the night:
Neatness counts.
Format counts.
Spelling counts.
Grammar counts.
Punctuation counts.
Diction counts.
Syntax counts.
Everything counts.

📧 An effective editor reads on behalf of <u>all</u> readers—
   and is equally hard to please.

📧 Always invite editors to comment on your work,
   and send a thank-you note when they do.

📧 If you receive similar comments on a piece of work
   from half a dozen readers, pay attention.

When you receive a rejection slip,
re-read your work with a fresh eye.
If it still pleases you, send it out again...the same day.

If the object is to create publishable writing,
it doesn't matter whether you generate
three rejections for every acceptance,
or three hundred.

Temper your enthusiasm over an acceptance
or your disappointment with a rejection.
Either way, it usually represents the opinion
of only one or two people.

◧ Ultimately you must trust your own judgement
(not that of the marketplace)
as to the worth of your writing.

◧ If you write it, there is a fair chance
it will be published.
If you do not write it,
there is no chance it will be published!

◧ For well-written work,
each rejection slip represents an error in marketing,
nothing more.

Each time you receive a rejection slip,
you are one step closer
to finding the right market for your work.

When you get a rejection slip,
congratulate yourself.
You can't get a rejection
unless you're writing
and marketing your work.

▭ Even commercially successful writers have finished
work for which they cannot find a publisher.

▭ If you continue to write and rewrite,
to market and re-market,
you will publish and re-publish.

▭ May your stride be longer
returning from the mailbox
than on the way to it.

- Respect what others know that you don't...
  especially about marketing.

- Marketing is always unfinished business.

- Of all the variables in marketing,
  the one over which the writer can exercise greatest
  control is the writing.

- If you write every day for a decade,
  you'll stand a good chance
  of becoming an overnight success.

The best salesperson for your book is you.
Not your agent,
not the publisher,
not the publisher's rep.
You.

Marketing your writing is no big thing.
It's a lot of little things.

Send all your finished work out to market
No fair hiding stuff in the drawer.

*I never had any doubts about my abilities. I knew I could write.
I just had to figure out how to eat while doing this.*

Cormac McCarthy

*Someday I hope to write a book where the royalties will
pay for the copies I give away.*

Clarence Darrow

Write for money or write for yourself,
   but make up your mind.

If you want to make money...
   write what needs to be written.

If you want to make money...
   write advertising copy, greeting cards, annual reports,
   speeches, policy manuals, instructional pamphlets...
   anything with a check attached to it.

For most writers, writing is the most fun they can have
   doing something for which they might be paid.

☞ Write what others need to have written
and you will always have a paycheck.
Write what you need to write
and you will always have a payoff.

☞ In writing...
many of the factors which determine commercial success
are beyond your control.
So focus on the factors you can control.

☞ In writing...
better too little than too much—
except for return postage.

John Steinbeck said,
"The profession of book writing
makes horse racing seem like a solid,
stable business."

If writing is to be your occupation,
it must be your preoccupation.

In publishing, the key question remains
"Who is going to buy this book?"

Small publishing houses are likely
to edit your book more carefully,
produce it more artfully,
and keep it in print longer.

In the small press there are no mid-list books.
Of necessity, every book is promoted.

✎   Never...
    argue with an editor over a rejection
    or a killed assignment.
    Save your ammo for arguing about the writing
    on the next assignment.

✎   Never...
    denigrate the publications in which your work
    has appeared—especially early work.

☞ Well-seasoned editors represent their readers effectively. That's how they got to be well-seasoned.

☞ Your writing may have been graded on a scale when you were in school, but with editors it's strictly pass/fail.

☞ Much of the editing and hand-holding once done by editors at large publishing houses is now done by agents and book doctors.

In submitting non-fiction,
always give your editor more than is expected,
by providing sidebars,
charts, ideas for graphics, photographs, et cetera.

Do not worry that editors might steal your work.
Why would they risk it,
when they can buy it on the cheap?

Some writers advise,
"Don't worry about having a literary agent:
by the time you need one,
they'll be all over you."
It's a lie!

Don't begrudge an agent his or her fee.
Really, would you want to do what an agent
does for a living?

Editors and agents
troll for new talent at writer's conferences.
Attend at least one a year and swim toward the bait.

Chapter Eleven
READING AND WRITING

Listen Like a Sponge, Read Like a Predator

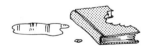

If you don't read for pleasure, you'll lose your edge as a writer.

Nora Roberts

There are worse crimes than burning books.
One of them is not reading them.

Joseph Brodsky

People love to look into others' lives—
especially if the others aren't aware of it.

The virtual reality created by the human mind
while reading is unmatched by any technology.

When a writer publishes a story,
he or she really publishes as many stories
as there are readers of that story.
Each reader creates the story anew,
based on his or her experience and attitudes.

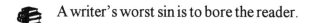 A writer's worst sin is to bore the reader.

Readers, bless them, will worry about almost anything. Be sure to give them something to worry about.

Readers of fiction want you to deceive them. All they ask is that you be good at it.

Read as a writer and write as a reader.

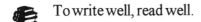 To write well, read well.

To grow as a writer, one must grow as a reader.

Read like an editor.
If you don't know how to read like an editor,
pretend you are a shopkeeper examining
a bill of sale.

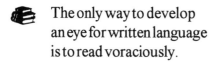

The only way to develop
an eye for written language
is to read voraciously.

Read the kind of writing you like to write.
<u>And</u> read stuff that is wildly different
from your usual interests.

Reading is never a waste of time,
especially for a writer.

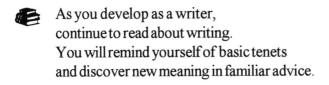

As you develop as a writer,
continue to read about writing.
You will remind yourself of basic tenets
and discover new meaning in familiar advice.

There is good and bad
in every piece of writing
but sometimes
you have to look a might hard
to find one or the other.

As you read, consider how the writer evoked
a response in you,
or motivated you to take action.

The writer who understands why people read
will understand how to write.

Reading shapes who we are;
writing shapes who we become.

Your body says, "You are what you eat."
Your mind says, "You are what you read."
Your soul says, "You are what you write."

Whether reading or writing,
a good book has a life
that won't let you live your own.

Revere the reader,
for the reader allows the writer access
to his or her most private domains:
the mind and the heart.

Listen like a sponge.
Read like a predator.

Chapter Twelve
THE WRITING LIFE
Everything Speaks to a Writer

The only thing I was fit for was to be a writer, and this notion rested solely on my suspicion that I would never be fit for real work, and that writing didn't require any.

Russell Wayne Baker

You write until you come to a place where you still have your juice and know what will happen next and you stop and try to live through until the next day when you hit it again.

Ernest Hemingway

Writing is a jealous mistress.

 The creative muse is nothing more than a nag,
and a possessive nag at that.

 What you wrote a year ago or a month ago
or yesterday
is now another writer's work.

In writing, as in everyday life,
people want you to be honest—
until you say things they don't want to hear.

 If you are concerned that your writing
may wound a friend or relative,
keep writing.
You are writing from the heart.

 Writers have friends, to be sure,
but mostly writers have sources.

Like everyone else, writers interpret reality.
Writers then manipulate their interpretations
in an attempt to define truth.

 As writers, we discover truths
about ourselves and others,
only to forget them.
And then, happily or not,
rediscover them.

The lower levels of your consciousness are far more honest than the upper levels. Trust your instincts.

 For a writer, "nothing" never happens.

 Nothing bad ever happens to a writer; it's all grist for the mill.

A writer is never <u>ever</u> off duty.

 Whoever said,
"No news is good news"
was not a writer.

 Your reputation as a writer
is re-defined with every piece you publish.

Understand life as well as you can,
so that your readers might live
with understanding
as well as they can.

 Write
in order to make sense
out of some aspect of your life
and you will likely do the same
for your readers.

 Writing fosters the illusion
that one can actually gain control over one's life.

Cranking your engine when you're out of gas
will only run down your battery.
Learn to accept that sometimes you need to refuel.

 Every writer endures this basic paradox:
whatever you write is wholly original
(a result of your particular experiences, attitudes,
knowledge and style)
and wholly unoriginal
(been done before, been said before, been written before).

 Every good writer is a sponge:
soak it up, wring it out.

In life and love and writing:
when one door closes, another opens.

 Unlike many skills,
writing often improves with age.

 Like the characters in The Wizard of Oz,
you will find within yourself
all you need to succeed as a writer.

Being a writer has two main advantages
and both of them are freedom.

 As with acting,
writing offers consummate freedom,
allowing exploration of the self
under the guise of character.

 As to writing as a career,
if you can take it or leave it,
leave it.

Nobody knows
what a writer is supposed to look like
or sound like or act like
until it happens.

 To experience burnout as a writer,
you must first have been on fire.

 Thank those who help you learn to write, of course—
and those who let you.

Stand in the rain
with your face turned upward,
every chance you get.

 Never...
take your professional relationships for granted—
not with editors, not with agents, not with publishers—
and certainly not with readers.

 Creativity is an undisciplined rascal,
always wanting to move on to the next thing,
never quite finishing the project at hand.

You can peek behind the refrigerator,
search the attic,
rattle through the junk drawer.
※ You won't find time for writing.

 As we grow older,
we continually re-invent our lives.
Writers pause to apply for copyrights along the way.

 To be a writer one must sentence oneself
to a life of solitary refinement.

For a writer,
school is never out.
Every time you sit down to write,
it's a take-home exam.

 Writing is sometimes like studying.
You sit there almost comatose
While nothing appears to be happening,
all hell may be breaking loose in your head.

 Everything speaks to a writer.

INDEX

PLASTIC
MODEL KITS

by

Jack C. Harris

CRESTWOOD HOUSE

New York

Maxwell Macmillan Canada
Toronto

Maxwell Macmillan International
New York   Oxford   Singapore   Sydney

Library of Congress Cataloging-in-Publication Data
Harris, Jack C.
    Plastic Model Kits / by Jack C. Harris. — 1st ed.
        p.   cm. — (Hobby guides)
    Includes index.
    Summary: Information about plastic model kits, how they originated, their components, how to put them together, how to display them, and how to join with other groups of modelmakers.
    ISBN 0-89686-623-8
    1. Models and modelmaking—Juvenile literature. 2. Plastics craft—Juvenile literature. [1. Models and modelmaking. 2. Plastics craft. 3. Handicraft.] I. Title. II. Series.
TT154.H27   1993
745.592'8—dc20
                                                                                                91-25201

Photo Credits
The author wishes to thank the following persons for their help in acquiring photographs for this book: Robert Fawler (diorama), Red Bank, NJ; Steve Garratano, Red Bank, NJ; Hobbymasters, Red Bank, NJ; Modelmakers of Southern Ocean County, Ocean County, NJ.

CRESTWOOD HOUSE

Macmillan Publishing Company
866 Third Avenue
New York, NY 10022

Maxwell Macmillan Canada, Inc.
1200 Eglinton Avenue East
Suite 200
Don Mills, Ontario M3C 3N1

Macmillan Publishing Company is part of the Maxwell Communication Group of Companies.

Produced by Flying Fish Studio

Printed in the United States of America

First edition

10 9 8 7 6 5 4 3 2 1

CONTENTS

THE EXCITING WORLD OF PLASTIC MODEL KITS

Have you ever stood in the stands cheering a superfast stock car on as it roars around the racetrack? Have you ever looked high in the air as a fighter jet streaks across the sky? Have you ever read the colorful and exciting adventures of a superpowered superhero? Have you ever sat spellbound watching a horror movie in which a mad scientist constructs an awesome monster?

If you've ever done any of these things, then you have probably also imagined yourself in the middle of an auto race, helping the pit crew tune the engine, fuel up the car, and rapidly change tires. You probably wished you could create the blazing engine of that fighter jet so its pilot could defend freedom around the world. Maybe you've even imagined creating your own superhero who puts on a cape and mask to go forth to fight crime and injustice. And maybe—just maybe—you've imagined yourself in the lab, carefully putting together the pieces of your own monster!

Just think what it would be like to build a monster...or a fighter jet...or a stock car...and yes, even a superhero. All you have to do is enter the thrilling and creative world of plastic model kits!

(photo left): You may become overwhelmed when you first enter a hobby or toy store to purchase a model.

5

Just after World War II, the first plastic model kits began to appear in stores around the country. They were simple scale reproductions of cars from the 1930s and earlier. Soon more complex kits were introduced, featuring scale models of things like fighter planes and historic ships.

By the late 1950s and early 1960s customizing car kits were on the market and a whole industry had sprung up around them. About the same time new modelmakers were introduced to the hobby with the appearance of plastic kits depicting famous movie monsters, superheroes, and vehicles from films and television shows.

Today plastic model kits are made to cover every subject. Some kits are really complex, while others strive for a simpler approach. Plastic model kits are practical for all ages and skill levels. This book will show you how easy it is to choose that first plastic model kit and start building it.

The book will also explain exactly what a plastic model kit is. You'll learn about the history of plastic model kits and explore the range of exciting models you can build, paint and display.

This book will show you the fun you can have in picking out and building plastic models. It will also help you select the right kit for you, as well as the necessary tools to do your building and the right paints so you can give your models a finished touch.

You'll also read about how to organize a plastic model kit club, how to display your models, and how to enter or organize a plastic model kit competition.

Building a plastic model can give you hours of fun. It's a hobby that is enjoyed by millions of people of all ages. Each model you build will be better than the last. Once you start, you'll find it's hard to stop.

WHAT IS A PLASTIC MODEL KIT?

A plastic model kit is exactly what it sounds like. It's a scale reproduction of a larger thing (car, plane, boat, for example), made of plastic pieces designed to be fitted together by the modelmaker. You can find kits in any hobby shop and in most toy stores. They usually come in cardboard boxes with a full-color photograph or painting on the top. The picture shows either a finished, painted model or a picture of what the model is based on.

No one is certain how the hobby of modelmaking began. For centuries engineers who were going to put up a building would first construct a miniature model. They would build these to scale so they could see exactly what the full-size structure would look like and how it would stand. Later, during the Industrial Revolution in the late 1800s, people would produce miniature working models of machines to make sure they would operate properly before building a real one.

All through history children have had smaller versions of adult machines as toys. Models of horses and wagons have been found in ancient houses. Model trains have been around since the first real trains clattered down the tracks. These models were not kits. They were made by parents for their children or by early toymakers. They were made from metal or wood.

When people learned to fly in the early 1900s, model planes quickly became popular. The first model planes were made of lightweight balsa wood, and each piece had to be cut by hand by the modeler. During World War II, scientists discovered plastic. They found that it was not only strong and durable but easy and inexpensive to manufacture. Toymakers saw plastic as the perfect material for model building kits. The first plastic kits on the market were of early cars. By the mid-1950s and early 1960s all kinds of different models became available. At the same time special modeling paints were made and sold along with the kits. No matter what the subject, there was a model kit to go along with it: Cars, ships, tanks, planes, superheroes, movie monsters, space vehicles, robots, knights in armor, horses, birds and more. That tremendous variety is still true today.

Creating a model for you to put together is a long process. A model company first decides what model to make. It might be a famous race car or a fighter jet that's in the news. Once the company has decided which model it is going to make, it buys the rights from whoever owns the original. It could be a movie company if it's a car from a film, or it could be the U.S. government if it's a fighter jet. The toy company's engineering staff then makes a scale drawing of the subject and creates a miniature in plaster. This is called a **prototype**. The plaster prototype is used to make metal **molds**. The metal molds are then finished by hand until every detail is accurate. With these metal molds the final plastic pieces are cast before being boxed in kits.

Once these finished boxed kits are shipped to your local hobby store, the fun begins for you. The excitement of plastic modelmaking is not only having a handsome model you can display, but in the hours of fun you can have by building it. And—even more exciting—you can go beyond the instructions to customize your model and make it one of a kind.

(photo right): Hobby store employees can be a big help when you are shopping for your first model.

CHOOSING YOUR FIRST PLASTIC MODEL KIT

When you first go into a store looking for a model, you may be overwhelmed. You will find boxed kits stacked from floor to ceiling in some stores. It will be very hard to decide which one to select.

You need some guidelines on choosing your first plastic model kit. In the early days, each of the plastic parts was molded in the same color. If you wanted your model to look like the original, you had to paint it with special paints. Naturally, painting your model was a big part of the fun. However, model manufacturers soon discovered that it takes practice to become good at painting models. Many inexperienced modelmakers were discouraged when their first try didn't turn out as they'd planned. They had trouble with the paints; they would also have difficulties gluing the pieces together and finally end up making a mess.

To help first-time modelmakers, the plastic kit manufacturers came up with **snap-together** models for beginners. These kits usually have different-colored plastic pieces, each piece already colored like the original. The pieces are designed to be put together easily with tiny plastic "tabs" that fit into specially sized holes. In other words, they "snap together."

If you are a beginner, you may want to consider getting such a model. Other than being **prepainted** and needing no glue, these plastic model kits are exactly like the more advanced kinds. You still have to read the instructions carefully, and you still have to find and fit each piece into place. Snap-together kits are a great way to become familiar with how plastic kits are constructed.

If you have not made any models, or if you've put together less than a dozen models, then you should look for **beginner** kits. Kits usually have a difficulty label on their boxes. Once you have completed between 13 and 50 kits, you should probably look for **intermediate** kits. Anything beyond that and you may be ready for an **advanced** kit.

The more advanced kits not only have more pieces, but they are designed to give the modelmaker a choice of pieces. These are called **customizing** kits. Many model car kits are designed like this. You can choose from among different engines to put in your car, as well as different hubcaps and other accessories. You should consider any customizing kit to be advanced.

Remember, once you select the kind of kit you want, you have to buy the proper equipment. If it's not a snap-together kit, you're going to have to buy glue and paints and brushes. In the next chapter you can read about the different kinds of tools and supplies you may need. If you have any questions while shopping, remember that the hobby store owner probably knows exactly what you're looking for and what you need.

Below is a convenient checklist of things to consider before you select any plastic model kit:

1. Decide on the kind of kit you want to put together. You can choose a car, a plane, a ship, an animal, a superhero

or anything else that interests you. The owner of the store can probably find exactly what you want.

2. Don't be misguided by the picture on the box. This shows the model in action. Instead, look for **built-up** samples of the model you have selected. There are probably completed models on display in the hobby store that will give you a better idea of what a finished model will look like.

3. Remember to buy a supply of the proper glues, paints and brushes to complete your model. Your hobby shop owner will be able to help you select all the correct materials and tools you'll need. If you're an intermediate or advanced modeler, you will probably have already accumulated much of what you'll need. Also your experience in assembling models and reading instruction sheets will tell you what's necessary to complete any plastic model kit.

4. Always rely on your local hobby shop owner for the answers to any other questions you might have about buying a plastic model kit.

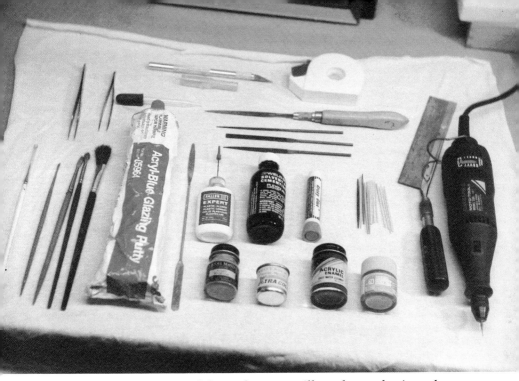

Before you put your model together, you will need some basic tools. Most of these can be found around your house or purchased at the local hobby store at reasonable prices.

YOUR MODEL TOOLS, GLUES AND PAINTS

Before you actually put together your model, you need some basic tools. Most of these can be found around your house or bought at your local hobby store at reasonable prices. You don't need them all to begin your hobby. The more advanced modelmakers use the more advanced tools. Here is a basic list of useful tools to have.

• The best brushes to use are camel hair or sable brushes, since model paints are enamel paints. It's a good idea to have a variety of widths for large areas and small details. Try to have one brush for each color and another one for mixing. Always clean your brushes immediately after each use with paint thinner, soap and water. They will be ruined if paint is allowed to dry on the bristles.

• There are a number of different kinds of model cement. Some thicker kinds come in tubes. Liquid cement comes with an applicator brush on the top. You should use white glue for cementing clear parts. Modeler's putty can be used for filling gaps if two pieces don't fit together exactly right. Use a thin metal spatula for spreading out and smoothing the putty.

• The electric grinder is a tool for more advanced model-makers. It is used to smooth down putty applications very quickly. If you're not careful, you could grind down too much of your surface. Beginners and intermediate modelmakers should use sandpaper.

• Tiny precision files are useful for smoothing away small bits of excess plastic. Emery boards can also be used for this purpose.

• Always make sure you have good lighting above your work space. A good reading lamp with a movable neck is the best kind to have.

• Tweezers can do most of the jobs that needle-nose pliers can do, but pliers have a better grip. These are good for holding and handling smaller parts that fit into tiny places.

• There are a wide variety of model paints. Some are basic sets in bottles. Some of these sets are especially mixed for military models or aircraft. They can be thinned and used in air brushes. The same colors also come in tiny spray cans. You should get a supply of paint thinner as well. Some of the paint sets come with their own bottle of thinner.

• Rubber bands are great for holding pieces together for a long time while the cement dries. These will also keep your hands free. When using rubber bands for the larger pieces, be sure you don't wrap them too tightly. The pressure can twist some pieces out of alignment.

• Sandpaper is excellent for smoothing away excess plastic and putty. You can buy this at a hobby or hardware store. Look for #200 to #600 sandpaper. These are the only grades that should be used on plastic. If you use a coarser grade, you could scratch the plastic surface. Lighter grades will do nothing more than polish the plastic. Remember not to sand too vigorously. This will cause heat from friction, which could destroy the detail on your model's delicate parts.

• Try to find both the flat and the round kind of wooden toothpicks. These should be used for applying glue to surfaces that are to be joined together.

• If possible, get a variety of tweezers. A standard pair is good for picking up and holding small parts. The kind with a spring or clip on them can hold pieces tightly, and you don't have to apply pressure yourself. Some tweezer clamps can be attached to your work table or desktop to act as a third hand.

• Utility knives with replacement blades come in a variety of sizes and are good for cutting and scraping away the excess plastic. Be certain you get a supply of replacement blades. Cutting plastic dulls the blades rapidly, and you should always use a sharp blade. Be careful! These blades are very sharp.

You should build your model in a large, well-lit work space with good ventilation.

PREPARING TO BUILD YOUR MODEL

Building a model kit takes some preparation. While each model is different, there are still some basic steps you should follow with every model. Below are eight steps that will get you started as soon as possible.

Step 1: *Preparing your work space.* You will need a large work space covered with newspapers. Make sure the surface is well protected, especially if it's a place where you do other work. Even with a covering of newspaper, paint and glue may soak through. It's important that you have plenty of light. A window with plenty of daylight coming through is good, but you should also have a desk lamp. The

18

best kind is one with a movable neck so you can aim the light where you want without disturbing your work surface. An area with good ventilation is important as well. Glue and paint fumes can be dangerous.

Step 2: *Reading the instructions.* When you first bring your model home, open it up and spread out the entire contents in front of you. The first thing you should look at is the instructions. These are usually prepared in step-by-step fashion and are illustrated with photos or line drawings. There will be a parts list numbering all the different pieces in your kit. Sometimes there will be a paragraph or two telling you about the history and background of the original, full-scale subject of your kit to build up your interest and excitement. Be sure to read the instructions completely before taking another step!

When you first bring your model home, open it up and spread the entire contents out in front of you.

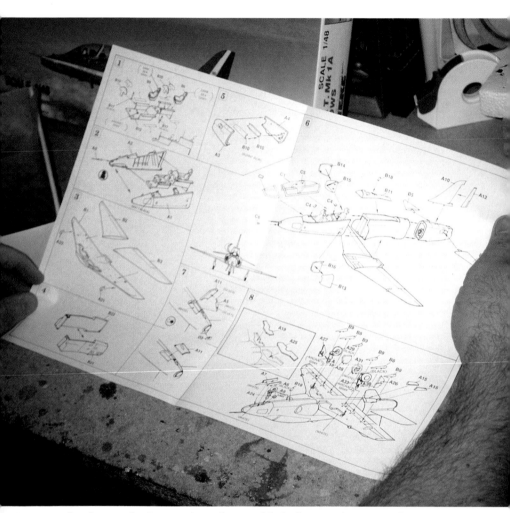

Look over the instructions thoroughly before getting started.

20

Step 3: *Examining your kit.* The next step is to examine the **trees**. The trees are plastic forms to which all the model pieces are attached. Examine these carefully against your instruction sheet parts list to make sure all the pieces are there and that none are broken. If some pieces have become separated from the trees, lay them aside carefully so they won't get lost. If any pieces are broken or lost, you can usually return the kit to the store where you bought it for a replacement. Be sure you keep your receipt to simplify the store exchange.

A kit may have a sheet with colorful decals for final details. Put the sheet aside for now. See page 34 for tips on applying decals.

Step 4: *Cleaning the pieces.* Next, wash all the trees in warm water with a little dishwashing liquid. This will remove any excess grease. Dry them with a hair dryer set on "cool." Don't use any heat, as this may warp your pieces. Store the dry pieces back in their box after you've blown out all the dust with the hair dryer. Let them dry completely for at least a couple of hours.

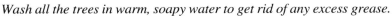

Wash all the trees in warm, soapy water to get rid of any excess grease.

Dry the trees with a hair dryer set on "cool," so as not to melt the delicate parts. Don't use any heat, as this may warp your pieces.

Flash is sometimes left on the trees. Very thin pieces of excess plastic are sometimes left over from the molding process. Remove these either by carefully breaking them off with a back-and-forth motion or by trimming them with your utility knife. Be careful not to remove or change any of the original shapes of the needed parts. Also be sure not to cut or break away any of the identifying numbers on the plastic trees.

Step 5: Prepainting. Your instruction sheet will tell you which pieces will need to be painted before they are removed from the trees. These are usually small pieces that would be difficult or impossible to paint once they are glued in place. Painting them while they are still attached to the tree will make them easy to hold and easy to dry.

Your instruction sheet will tell you which pieces need to be painted before they are removed from the trees.

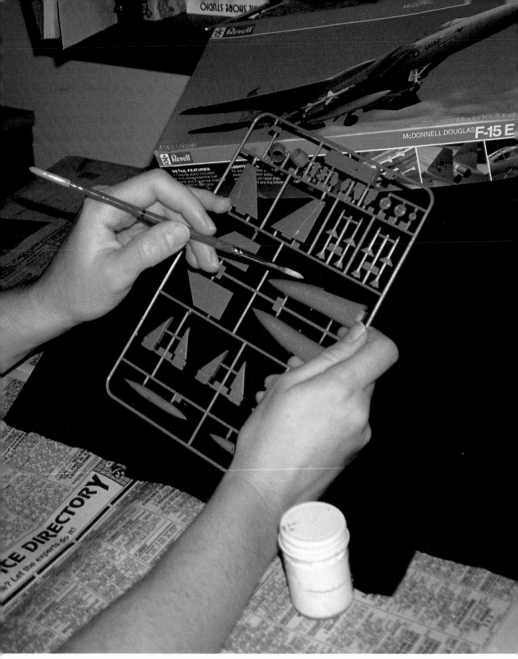

Painting the small pieces while they are still attached to the tree will make them easy to hold and easy to dry.

Step 6: *Removing the pieces from the trees.* Once all the prepainted pieces are dry, you can remove pieces from the trees as you are ready to use them. Never remove a piece until you need it. Remove them in the order given in the instructions. The best way to remove them is by using a very sharp utility knife. When cutting, lay the tree down flat on your tabletop or on a hard cutting block. Cut the tree a fraction of an inch from the part first. Then you can trim the tree from the part, being careful not to cut any of the part itself. If there is a little of the tree still attached, you can sand it smooth with a piece of sandpaper. Again, be careful not to sand too much or you'll change the shape of the part. If a part is small, it might be easier to hold if you use a pair of tweezers.

If you break the part, immediately glue it back together and let it dry. If you can't glue it, look on the instruction sheet to see if you can order a replacement part from the manufacturer. If you bend a part out of shape, you can heat it up slightly with a heater or in an oven until it is soft. Then you can bend it back into place. If this is necessary, be sure to have an adult's supervision! Fumes from melting plastic can be very, very dangerous! Also, if your part is clear or chrome, don't try to use heat to reshape it (see *Step 8*).

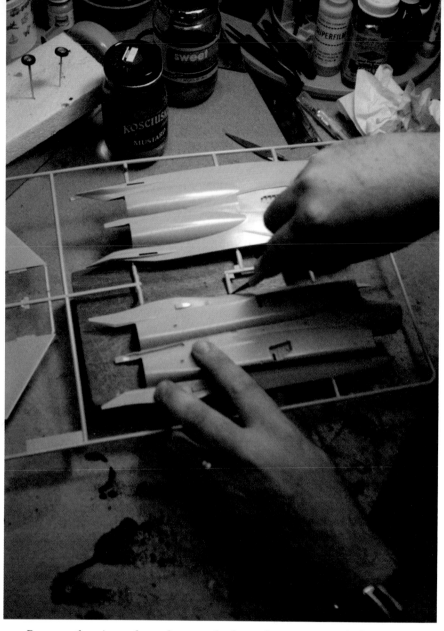

Remove the pieces from the trees in the order recommended in the instructions.

Before gluing, test the fit of each piece. If it doesn't fit properly, you may have to sand it or bend it into proper alignment.

Step 7: *Prefitting the pieces.* Before gluing, test-fit each piece. If it doesn't fit properly, you may have to sand it or bend it into proper alignment. Sometimes it's easier to glue the parts and then sand down extending defects. Just remember to do this carefully so you won't mar any surface details. You can also use model putty to fill in cracks and spaces. See page 31 for details.

Step 8: *Special chrome and clear parts.* Chrome and clear parts should be treated differently from all others. Chrome parts have to be specially prepared before gluing. These parts look like chrome because the manufacturer has actually coated them with a thin sheet of metal. You have to sand off this metal coating from any surface that has to be glued. The glue won't work on the metal, only the plastic. You can also scrape it off with a sharp knife. Keep your chrome pieces in a safe place so they won't get scratched.

You have to be extremely careful with clear parts. These are usually the parts of the kits that represent windows or canopies. If they are scratched or if glue gets on their surfaces, they will be ruined. If you do scratch a clear part, here's how you can repair it. First, coat the piece with petroleum jelly. Then carefully apply a thin layer of clear fingernail polish. When that is dry, apply another coat of the polish. Repeat this process every couple of hours, until the layers of dried polish are as thick as the original clear piece. If you're careful not to let any air bubbles form, you'll have a perfect replacement piece.

Now you're ready to begin to put your model together.

(photo left): Chrome parts are easily scratched, so keep them in a safe place until they are ready to be used.

ASSEMBLING YOUR PLASTIC MODEL KIT

The first rule is to follow the directions in the exact order in which they are given. The designers have made sure their directions will enable you to fit all the pieces and sections in the proper sequence.

Gluing. When you assemble a plastic model kit, gluing is the most important step. It's also the step you'll have to do most often. Most model glues are alike, but some work better than others in different temperatures and on different plastic surfaces. You may have to use a few different brands before finding the one you like best.

When using glue from a tube, remember to clean the cap out occasionally. Otherwise built-up glue will eventually prevent you from replacing the cap. Always replace the cap on the tube, or the glue will dry up rapidly. Also, model cement is very flammable. Don't use it near heat or an open flame. And make sure the room has proper ventilation.

When gluing pieces, squeeze out a tiny blob of glue onto a small scrap of paper. With a wooden toothpick, apply a small amount of glue to both surfaces that are to be joined. Allow them to dry for a few minutes before pressing them together. Hold them in place with a tweezer clamp or rubber bands. The glue actually melts the plastic so that it joins together. This is why you should use very small amounts and try not to get any on surfaces that are not to be glued. Properly glued parts should be dry in about an hour, but you should really wait a full day to make sure. As the first sections dry, you can continue working on other sections that need to be glued.

Clear pieces can be glued with white glue. The white glue can be wiped away with a damp cloth if it gets on other surfaces.

Liquid glue works best if there are no gaps between the connected surfaces. If there are gaps, there is more of a chance the liquid cement will leak on pieces you want to keep clean. Like the tube glue, you should wait a day before doing any more work on liquid- or white-glued pieces.

Putty. If gaps show between glued pieces once they are dry, you can use your putty to fill them. Use toothpicks to apply the putty on smaller gaps and a metal spatula for larger gaps. Let the putty dry and sand it smooth with an electric grinder or #600 sandpaper. Blow off all the excess dust before you try painting the puttied surface.

Painting. When painting your model, mix a tiny amount of thinner and paint in the paint bottle cap. Don't let it get so thin that it runs, but it shouldn't be so thick that it blobs up and obscures surface details. Paint one color at a time, using long, smooth paint strokes in one direction. Clean your brush when you're finished.

Paint one color at a time, using long, smooth strokes in one direction. Clean your brush when you're finished.

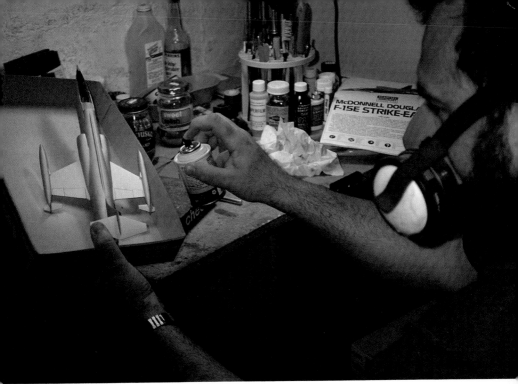

When using spray cans, make sure you have good ventilation. This modeler wears a filter mask for additional protection from paint fumes.

If you're using spray cans, it's best to have a ventilator booth. A ventilator booth is a big metal device with an opening in one end large enough to hold your model. The other end has a powerful fan that draws paint fumes and excess paint out of your workroom. If you don't have such equipment, paint outdoors on a calm day with no breezes. Using masking tape, cover all surfaces not to be painted. Spray just as if you're using a brush, with long strokes in one direction. If you're using an air brush, use the same method, applying even pressure at all times. Clean all equipment as soon as you've finished each color. Let the paint dry for a full 24 hours before applying a second coat (if needed) or further assembling the piece.

Decals. Trim decals with scissors as close to the edge of the decal as possible. If you're experienced, you can use your utility knife for this. Soak the decal in warm water with a little dishwashing liquid until it is loosened from the sheet. Using tweezers, remove it from the water and apply it in place. With a dry paper towel, dab the decal from the center to the edges until there are no air bubbles.

Be sure to trim the decals as close to the edge as possible.

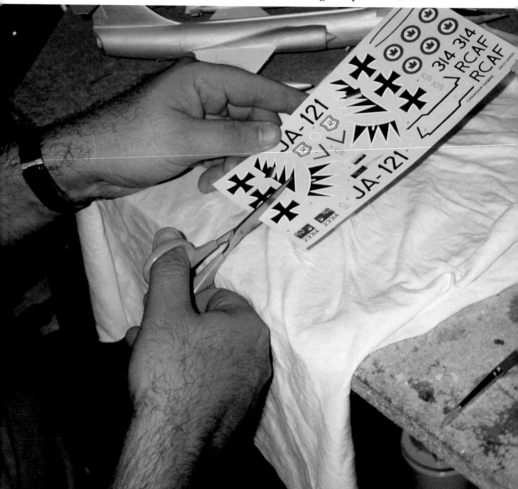

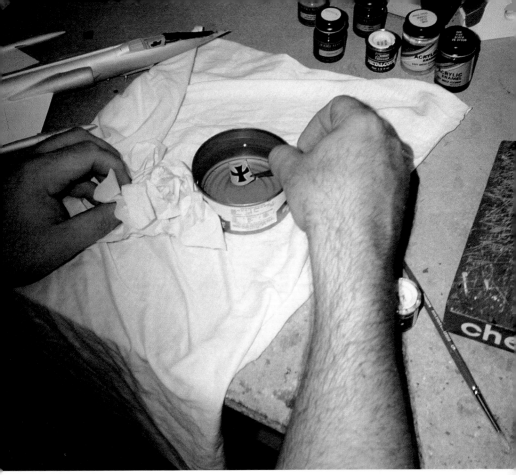

Soak the decal in warm, soapy water until it loosens from the sheet.

Don't hurry. Let everything dry longer than you think necessary. Carefully think about each step before you actually perform it. A mistake in gluing or painting can sometimes completely ruin your efforts. Building models correctly will take a long time. One of the main reasons for assembling plastic model kits is to have a good time for a long time!

Modelers keep large libraries of reference materials. These books can help you make your models look accurate as well as give you background information on the type of model you're building.

CUSTOMIZING YOUR PLASTIC MODELS

Some kits, as mentioned earlier, are customizing kits. This means they give the builder options on how to complete the plastic model. Advanced modelmakers don't consider such kits "real" customizing. They say that actual customizing happens when you take your model beyond the instruction sheet by creating changes that will make your model unique.

Always save the extra parts you receive in your model kits. You can use them later to customize future models.

The most common way of doing this is by adding accessories and touches of your own. Advanced modelmakers create extra pieces out of wood or scraps of plastic from other models. Using their utility knives, they cut plastic pieces of their own and add them to their finished models. They might put extra chrome on car models. They might put more weapons on their military models.

Painting is another way of customizing. Making up your own color scheme rather than following the one in the instructions can give your model its own look. Some modelmakers **weatherize** their cars and planes, making them look old or used by painting them that way. They may use colored pieces of chalk for rust marks and real mud to make the vehicle look as if it had traveled hard. They may even melt a wheel to give a car a flat tire.

Once you've become an advanced modelmaker, you'll discover all kinds of different methods of customizing. When you become a master at it, people looking at your models will think your customized changes were how the model was originally supposed to look. Customizing is one of the "extras" in modelmaking.

A MODELMAKING CLUB

One of the best ways to gain experience in model-making and to get new ideas is from a modelmaking club. Many hobby stores have organized modelmaking clubs, and members meet in the store to construct models together. People who run the store may hold classes for beginners and give demonstrations around the community.

Schools sometimes have clubs too, and so do scout troops and local libraries. Check out each of these locations for information on modelmaking clubs. Even if these groups don't sponsor their own clubs, they probably know where one is located and can help you contact it. If not, check out local community bulletin boards and classified sections in the newspaper. Many clubs advertise their meetings and activities through these outlets.

If none of this helps you locate a club, you might want to put an ad in the newspaper or on a bulletin board yourself. Such an ad might look like this:

BEGINNING MODELMAKER
LOOKING FOR A MODELMAKING CLUB
PLEASE CONTACT:
(YOUR NAME)
(YOUR PHONE NUMBER OR ADDRESS)

You might also want to form your own club. You can put a different ad in the newspaper or on a bulletin board that could look like this:

MODELMAKING CLUB BEING FORMED
BEGINNERS, INTERMEDIATES & ADVANCED
MODELMAKERS WELCOME
FOR INFORMATION, CONTACT:
(YOUR NAME)
(YOUR PHONE NUMBER OR ADDRESS)

Along with making models and giving classes and demonstrations, clubs can sometimes share the costs of expensive equipment that would be hard for you to afford by yourself. For instance, a club could own an air brush and an air compressor that all members could use. They also might be able to rent work space where everyone could work together or individually.

Modelmaking is a hobby that can be enjoyed by one person or a large group. And being a member of a modelmaking club is a great way to make new friends and learn more about plastic model kits.

(photo left): Modelmaking clubs are a great way to get together with other enthusiasts to exchange ideas and pick up tricks of the craft from more experienced modelmakers.

DISPLAYING YOUR PLASTIC MODELS

Most plastic model kits come with a stand for displaying your finished model. This is especially true with plane and ship models. More advanced modelmakers like to display their models more dramatically. Hobby shops sell plastic boxes specially designed for models. These cover the model completely. You can see the model but it is also protected from dust.

Aviation modelmakers often use thin piano wire or fishing line to suspend their models from the ceiling. This makes their planes look as if they are in flight. The same method is used for superhero models to make them seem to be flying overhead.

Some modelmakers build **dioramas** around their finished kits. Dioramas are miniature settings. For instance, a model car fan will build a miniature racetrack section, with spectator stands and lane markers to make the car look as if it's actually in a race. Jet modelmakers may build a miniature of an airfield, with technicians all around. Those making military models sometimes build battlefields to display their tanks or jeeps. Modelmakers make alien landscapes for their robot to stalk across. Hobby shops sell separate scale figures for such dioramas. Modelmakers use miniature trees and foliage designed for model railroads to make their dioramas look more realistic. Sometimes real rocks and soil are used for further realism. Cotton is used for

smoke. Tiny, battery-powered electric light bulbs are sometimes used to illuminate model dioramas. Like customizing,
dioramas are limited only by the modelmaker's imagination.

A good display can make your model look all the more
impressive. And building a diorama can sometimes be even
more fun than making the model itself. And a display case
for your diorama can be made from a fish aquarium!

*Dioramas are miniature settings in which modelmakers place their
finished products.*

PLASTIC MODEL KIT COMPETITIONS

Many hobby stores hold periodic modelmaking contests. There are usually different age classes, depending upon experience. Trophies are often awarded, along with free kits or discounts at stores or even cash prizes and scholarships.

Many regional and local contests are organized by the **International Plastic Modelers Association (IPMS),** the main national organization for people interested in plastic modelmaking. Many of the members are hobby store owners. The IPMS holds a national contest every year, with categories covering just about every type of modelmaking. There are also age categories from children to adults, and skill categories from beginner to advanced. The contests are held in local stores, with each store's winner being entered into national competition. Ask your local hobby dealer for further details on IPMS contests.

The contestants' models are usually on display for many weeks. These displays give the beginner an excellent opportunity to see the results of more advanced modelmakers. Contests also heighten the thrill and fun of plastic kit modelmaking.

(photo left): Contests are often held by hobby stores for modelmakers of all ages and levels of experience.

FOR MORE INFORMATION

The following list will provide additional information about plastic model kits.

Kalmbach Books publishes three books for plastic modelers which must be ordered by product number:

The Art of Diorama by Ray Anderson.
    Product number: 12080
Hints and Tips for Plastic Modeling by Burr Angle.
    Product number: 12045P
Building Plastic Models by Robert H. Schleicher.
    Product number: 12027P

All orders should be sent to:
    Kalmbach Books
    P.O. Box 1612
    Waukesha, WI 53187

You can also write to:
    International Plastic Modelers Association (IPMS)
    P.O. Box 2890
    Sacramento, CA 95812-2890

GLOSSARY

advanced—A modelmaker who has assembled 50 or more plastic model kits.

beginner—A modelmaker who has assembled 12 or fewer plastic model kits.

built-up—A plastic model kit that has been assembled and is used in a hobby store for display purposes.

customizing—Adding details on a plastic model kit that are not included in the original instructions.

diorama—A three-dimensional setting representing a typical surrounding scene in which modelmakers display their finished kits.

flash—Bits of excess plastic on the edges of pieces in a plastic model kit.

intermediate—A modelmaker who has made more than 12 plastic model kits but less than 50.

IPMS—International Plastic Modelers Association, the organization for modelmakers.

mold—The frame on or around which a model is made.

prepainted—A plastic model kit made from different-colored pieces so it does not need painting.

prototype—A scale model of a car, boat, plane, or other vehicle, made of plastic, from which plastic model kit molds are made.

snap-together—A plastic model kit requiring no glue.

tree—The plastic posts to which pieces of plastic model kits are attached when the kit is first opened.

weatherizing—Detail painting to make models appear more realistic by making them look "used."

INDEX